life dealer

First published in Great Britain in 2022 by Turqoise Quill Press
an imprint of Not From This Planet

Copyright © 2022 by Catriona Messenger
Cover Design by madappledesigns
Illustrations by Catriona Messenger
Formatting by The Amethyst Angel

ISBN: 978-1-912257-62-1

First Edition

life dealer

Poetry & Illustrations
by
Catriona Messenger

Turquoise
Quill
Press

Also by Catriona Messenger

hope dealer

Walking together

How blessed I am
With Family and Friends

Leaps of faith

You are courageous
In your leaps of faith
Knowing your desire for change
But you do not know
Where Life is going
Yet bravely you follow
Trusting Life *does* know…

You seem to be missing

Every day that's here
And heightened some days
The aching confusion of loss
Though sure there must be more
To this world than meets our eyes
More to this, than our senses can provide
Limited as we are, in a physical way
Much more than these bounds can say
And sadly, I do see today
The empty chair
Hollow space where you used to be seen
And heard
And touched…
And we continue to miss you
And grieve you

In this limited view
And that hurts
Yes, this narrow view
Our physical perception, can so painfully hurt
But let us give to ourselves and remember
The Happiness given by you
Every precious recognised moment
And choose to notice that too
Providing ourselves with Love
Love, I'm sure you still sustain
Maybe unseen, unheard and untouched
But still very much
Gifted by you
And merely outside our limited view

Wrong

Wrong?
Being ourselves
Impossible to be
Anything other
How could it be?
That we could get
Being ourselves
Wrong!

Worth it

Agents of Worth are everywhere
bringing messages in spoken words
and abounding eyes. Facial expressions
and compelled physical actions
Presents falling onto our needy laps
and into our willing hands
supporting our chosen path
laying out its cobbles under our feet
Agents of Love disguised by perception
their messages misunderstood
and wrongly judged, but always hitting
the mark, the spot, the targeted asking
The gift that is wanted for the path
to lay down its route. Agents leaving signs
written in wrinkles, dyed in cloth
clues in the nectar of smells
Words understood and written confusion
spoken, unspoken, heard, unheard
Energetic agreements in sparring, warring
and making love, mirrors that don't lie
Agents of Life find us, love us exactly
how we ask to be found and loved
Our wonderous collaboration on earth
in universe, in mind, in wonder

Flow

With broken hearts
  we grow
In broken hearts
 New blood has to
    flow . . .

Thoughts

Who am I
If I don't believe
My own thoughts
Who am I
If I acknowledge
My emotions are not truth
They are responses
To my thoughts

Where

Where man sees chaos
God does not
Where she sees wrongness
Peace does not
Where ego sees vanity
Whole does not
Where brain sees problems
Life does not
Where thinking sees loss
Knowing does not

Label

When
there
is
no
label
to
define
us
what
are
we?
nothing
or
everything
or
both?

What more can I be?

Not who you really are – I remind myself
This behaviour – not who I really am
Learned, observed strategies
Are they serving me well?
What lives beyond this mistaken identity?
Not who I really am
Watch…
With Love…
Watch my personality at play
I'm asking to leave automatic behaviour behind
Reaching for the gracious part of me
Richer than survival
More powerful than fuel for fear
Bigger than flesh and bones
Beneficial to the world
The saviour is acknowledgment
Fall in love with willingness
To see this vulnerable human being
That I think I am

Held by something greater
Holding, with patience, waiting to be known
Always there beyond a pause
Start looking
Everywhere
Opportunities to ask and see
What more can I be in all of this?

Together

When humble arrives
Something special
Tunes in
Contentment joins
Tea is served
In china cups
And all can
Sip and
Slurp
Together

-Delicious

Blessings

What if…
What if it's *All* a gift

What if

What if life is different
to how we think it is
and it's our thinking
that gets in the way
obscuring a different life
what if we stop…
we explore…

what else might be seen
and heard…
and shown…
what if…
we become explorers
of our currently unknown…

Gifts

what if Death carries in its hands
more gifts than Life ever could

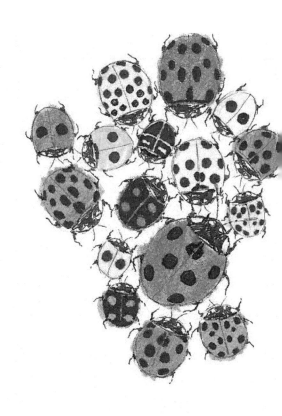

Different

What if
compromises
aren't that at all
what if they are
simply a different view
another experience

What All

All is possible
When I imagine limitless
When I exist in All
Visiting moments of this truth
That All possibilities exist
What if I decide to see
Other versions of reality
What if I decide to be flexible
Open to seeing more possibilities
What if I really choose to believe
In magic and miracles
Knowing that magic and miracles
Are the flexibility to see more
To believe something other
Willingness to let go of agreements
In seeing a particular limited view
Saying yes to emptying this vessel
Of ancient narratives
Allowing the unthinkable, the
Unimaginable to show up
What's possible beyond the beliefs
Of what's possible
Embracing, All is possible

Experience

I'm having an experience
And more than that I do not know
I'm having an experience
And other than that I do not know
I'm having an experience
And beyond that I do not know

Wee Lizard

Stop trying and just be
Says this lizard to me
Appearing at my side
With scaly skin
And a slithering tongue
New life already begun
And all the tails you lost
Are tales you might just tell
All mixed up, in heaven and hell
Regrowth yes already begun
Secrets might carry
on that slithering tongue
Rest here til you know
Quite who you've become
Pause just here a while
In this generator sun

Wee Bee

Bee on blossom
Busy buzzing
Collecting
Communicating
If I'm listening
I hear
Life is beautiful
Yes, I can fill myself up
With Awe
To Love my world

Fog

We can get a bit lost in our own fog

others help *lift* the edges of **our heavy blanket**

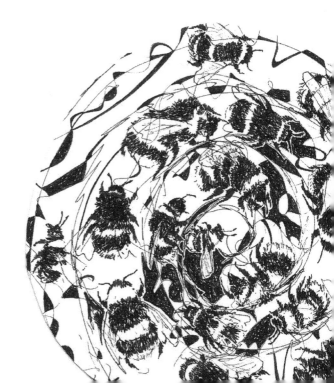

Unravel?

Unravelling
but what really is there
to unravel
stuff of life
I chose to believe
many things
I've given a life
in truth
not alive at all
an inside world
an inside me
all Imagined
no-thing
to unravel

Tired

what are you?
weighing me
down
wearing thinness
in my enthusiasm
the unexpressed
lays heavy
hard
to carry

Thin Places

Are they more magical places
Closer to Spirit, closer to God
To our Truth, the I AM in me
We seek them out, these Thin Places

Holding them separate and special
What if…
Special and Thin, encompass us all
Holding us all days, Always

Do we only acknowledge Ethereal
When boxes are ticked
When images and words match
Confirm what we've chosen, to believe

Boxes we're checking around Spirit
About God, defining Connection
With Truth, our Worth, our Love
What if

We cease resisting God in All
And listening to our limiting beliefs
Throw out these finite ideas we've drawn
What if

We experience the Empyrean
On the train, at this desk
Walking the pavement and ordering lunch
What if

We allow the Divine in pain
Through discomfort and conflict
Seeing Thin Places in enemies
Not just friendship, silence and peace

What would change
If Rarefied is experienced
Thin is carried with us
Holding us Always, all days

The Wasp

I hear your approach
With your menacing vibration
WHY? I hear inside myself
Are you necessary to creation?

As my judgment flares
We become set apart
Then your interest in me
Does fly off the chart!

This emotion - it's an anxiety
But could it be a guiding light?
Where judgment sits tight
There will be freeze, fight or flight

Whose sting will be worse?
Mine or yours. Exasperation
Deep breath… go inside
Choose my stance, my situation

A new perspective could meet my needs
Quietly… I appreciate your worth
Your actions match and
You - gently - leave

You were my teacher
            Connected to my grace
                    The wasp and me…
                            We can share this space

Poems

This isn't a perfect poem exercise
It's a tangle of ink and paper
Creatively exhibiting together
Words that I interact with
In a vain attempt to describe
Energy in my awareness
That's verily indescribable

The River

The River was calling me everyday
Showing me, I was asking in everyway
Fallen in the trap, that causes our woe
Believing in limits to what I could know

Speaking these limits, my fears, my needs
My heart pulled away, refusing to concede
It knew of Love where we really belong
Hearing the flow in the sweet River song

You stood upstream and my life felt hard
I couldn't follow my heart with you in charge
The River song came louder with its call
My struggle with you began to wane, to fall

Letting go, wanting the River's path
The sun bathing me with its loving grasp
And now I understood there is heaven on earth
I could touch true Love and what that's worth

Love was all and all is good
… I wish to fill this life
With the River's song,
of heavenly Love

The meeting

One moment
In meeting
A connection
Beyond words
Just awareness
Of shared
Presence
And there you are
In my heart
And I in yours
Acknowledged or not
This is the truth
Precious and held
In the warmth
Of healing our separation
Don't spoil this
With your words

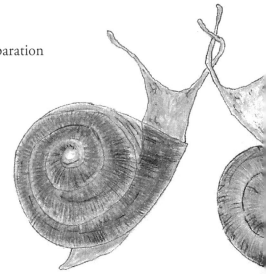

Don't push against this
With your fears
Don't show up as less
Than this deserves
Find the best of you
In me
And the best of me
In you
As important
As each other
This meeting is ours
To give and receive
As many gifts
As we are willing
To share
In meeting

Peace

The greatest peace, I know
Is clear, in words unknown

The gold

Was gentle movement
Redirection, a simple turn

Everything else spoken
Was surrounding flotsam

The glean of the Sun
Illuminated the crest
Of my Original Wave

The fix

Do you think
I can stop
trying to fix this
and embrace it all
instead?

The concept of One

As One
To be at One with
Nature
Self
Others
The Divine
To be at One with
Surely, cannot exclude
To be One, is to be all
Everything
This world
And beyond
Can we pick
And choose
What we are
At One with
Or to truly
Experience
The experience of One
Surely all is included
To be truly felt
As One

The Caldew

My river of many places and faces
Sure, I will never tire of you
Playing out your rhythm
For contemplation as you do

I've watched you from afar
Bowscale fell my seat
I've sat where another loosens itself
Where you and the river Roe meet

I delight in spaces you constantly change
Eroding banks, moving swells of stone
I trust in you, whenever I seek you
That my melody will match your own

My family have played and paddled in you
Collected pottery you're taking to sea
Fished for tiddlers and built a dam
Dipped toes with picnics and flasks of tea

Your tones are many and stocked with flow
Freedom, destruction, shallow and deep
Carrier of life from your depths to your banks
Broad, sleepy and steady, rapid, raucous and steep

And when I wake and all has changed
And confusion sits troubling me
I find myself looking to rest with you
Playing your acoustic and singing - 'just be'

The beech trees petition

Oh leave this barren spot to me
Share woodman spare the Beechen tree
Though bush or floweret never grow
My dark, unwarming shade below
Nor summer bud perfume the due
Of rosy blush or yellow hue
Nor fruits of autumn blossom born
My green and glossy leaves adorn
Nor murmuring tribes from me derive
In ambrosial amber of the hive
Yet leave this barren spot to me
Spare woodman, spare the beechen tree
Thrice twenty summers I have seen
The sky grow bright the forest green

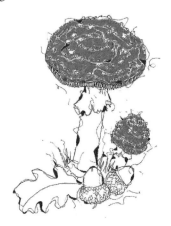

And many a wintry wind have stood
In bloomless, fruitless solitude
Since childhood in my rustling tower
First spent it's sweet and sportive hour
Since youthful lovers in my shade
Their vows and faith of rapture made
And on my trunks surviving frame
Carved many a long-forgotten name
Oh by the sighs of gentle sound
First breathed upon this sacred ground
By all that love hath whispered here
On beauty heard with ravished ear
As loves own alter honour me
Spare woodman, spare the beechen tree

By James Crocket

Still

And I'll cry some tears in the morning
And sometimes before I sleep
Still sometimes in the middle of the day
Forever broken hearted
I will always need to weep

What changes is being ok with bleeding
Becoming accustomed to feeling
Joy and pain together
Celebration and mourning are tethered

Happiness and sorrow are joined
Forgiveness and guilt have a bond
Acceptance and resistance embrace the stay
An open wound that still walks anyway

Stored Life

What I store inside me
Paints a picture
Of my world
Sometimes
I notice
I want to clear a shelf
And choose
Something else
Instead

Searching

What is there
When the seeking
Wobbles in weariness
Trembles with exhaustion
Knowledge becomes tiresome
Mystics and Masters
All look the same
And hum as we all do

What is there
When meaning drips and melts
Seemingly distorted
And agitation
Waxes and wanes with Peace
Like tumbling pebbles
Pulled by the tide
Creating sand

What is there
Beyond the desire
To understand
To find…
Whatever seemed
To be lost…
Substituting the unknown
What is there beyond
Searching…

Worlds

Sand Martins Alive
Bountiful River
Border Terrier Paddling
Heart-full
Magical Sun
Patterned Shade
Resonant Nature
Blanketed with Silence
Deeply Drenched Love
Easy!

Loved Ones Dead
No Water to Drink
Ragged Bone Strays
Heart-ache
Burning Sun
Desperate Shadows
Violent Noise
Carpeted Suffering
Deeply Drenched Fear
Help!

Salar

A thousand miles to travel to the pool where she was spawned,
A hundred rocky falls she'll leap and a hundred more beyond.
Tired as a weary pilgrim; rheotropism guides her course
Through high and frothing cataracts,
fearsome the water's force.

Her journey almost mastered; the last leap; only one,
She's tossed and thrown back in the foam,
her courage almost gone.
The turbulent pool is deep and cool,
Those bruises it does soothe
Then one brave effort gains her goal the nursery of her youth.

Her eggs she sheds
Her strength is spent;
Her species safe she dies content.
So high a price she's had to pay,
but nature can be cruel that way,
Inert she floats where life began,

And Life Begins All O'er Again.

By Ellen Black

Rivers

River of Salty Tears
Perspiration of Grief

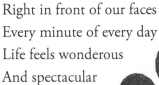

Moments

Really important
Life-changing moments
Big and small
In truth without hierarchy
And happening under our noses
Right in front of our faces
Every minute of every day
Life feels wonderous
And spectacular
When I notice

46

Procrastination

all communication
a moment for exploration
  the message of procrastination

Stress

 what is this stress
what is its purpose
 guiding me somewhere else
away from something unwanted
  guidance about avoidance

Of Healing

 of moving past painful
to new ground
 but not unknown
  telling me what I see
is something other
  than I am

the Real me

Pain

Not what we
think it is?

Ol' boots

Ol' boots
your conversations with the earth
have worn you out
creased for worthiness
Now, you let Water in…

Noticing me

I love you
Acknowledging it now?
As I drift on my ocean
Of silence
Silent but
For the caress
Of lazy waves
The beat and whoosh
Of wings
And calls
Of delight
In this endless blue
Shutting my eyes
To rest…
I see my dark too
All perceived
As I choose it to be
I love you

Narrated world

Sometimes I wish
To never speak again
To never hear again
That which comes
Out of mouth
Sounding like
A twisted mess
Hypocrisy
Even when
We're sure it's not
Convinced it's true
Still laced
With contradiction
Is there only
One possible way
Of unravelling
A narrated world
Is it
To never
Speak again

Needs

My serenity
and the dishes.
I don't want
my serenity
to rely
on someone else
doing the dishes

My Self Talk

Talk to yourself in helpful ways
It doesn't have to be true
What is truth anyway
When we all have different opinions
Different beliefs
Truth resides in silence
And that is helpful indeed
But talk can be helpful
Thoughts can be helpful too
Spoken in your head
Can be there to build your strength
Helping you move
From dis-ease to ease
Healing the old and letting go
Creating ground for something new
Creating space for change
Adaptation and flexibility
Responding to life with love
Responding to yourself with love
What you bring in
For yourself
Can then be given out

All of Life

My prayer is my silent reverence
There is nothing that isn't as it is to be
And nothing that does not astound me

My own illusion

Weightless in this heavy jar
My own prison
Transparent as if not there
But when I try to expand
The glass walls dunch me
Restrict me
Like I'm taxidermy
On some museum shelf
With ancient agreements
To live this way

What happens when I am roused
The ignited lover, fractures
These silica walls
Those archaic rules
Another time
Designed for someone else
I'm weightless in this heavy jar
I'll not be held forever
I'll not be fooled much longer
By transparent limitations
My own prison
I'll be weightless
Beyond this heavy jar

This life

My meditation
This life
I'm experiencing
Giving my attention to

My meditation
This world
I focus in
And receive

My meditation
This dream
I'm giving to
Reflecting my thoughts

My meditation
Always
Each moment
Of my attention

Compost

My compost
my pain
and trauma
hurt
anger
all twisted parts
of me

these distortions
held to decay
and rot
what nourishment
it is
when I give it up
and it's recycled

feeding the earth
under foot
giving life to
energetic soil
cultivating
creating
something else

This world

The world is my Church,
Standing at this altar each day
Laying down my experiences as offerings
Taking new blood and fodder for the coming
Led blindly by constantly flowing Mercy
Wisdom that orchestrates behind the scenes
Filtering through cells, vibrating, speaking
This is truth – all this creation

My brain

My brain believes whatever I tell it
Hey then…
Listen to myself and check
What am I telling it…

Fuel

My anger is fuel
For my expansion
Becoming more
Boon
For growth
That matches
The abundance of
My perceived loss

Mother Wolf

With pounding heart, I speed
And with heaving chest, I gasp
The air wrenched in
I must endure
Or my pups, they will not last
The calf from herd, we have coerced
For his mother, his voice is shrill
A shriek of fear, he bolts chaotic
We shall break his will
We move on him, it is not long
Defeated his courage gives in
No mother came to rescue him
He is forsaken, it is our win
As we bring him down, I hear his pain
His fear consumes my heart
My pack tears at his flesh and bones
Broken from his soul, I played my part
I stand still heaving, for want of air
And behold this calf's demise
The cry's now silent
The air is still
Grey cloud of death across his eyes
I have to choose my pups or theirs
My chest aggrieved for his mother's loss
I will protect my pups; their life is mine
I resolve to feed them - at any cost!

There's NO monster under MY bed!

It's true, I've looked, there's no monster under there
Just my slippers, a book and my teddy bear
Erikka, have you checked under your bed?
NO... because monsters aren't real Erikka said!

Are you sure, I thought I saw one last night
Waiting under my bed to give me a fright
He looked green and hairy with great big feet
I thought that's the kinda monster I don't want to meet!

I'll look under again – he's not there tonight
Perhaps he's hiding out of sight
Oh, Ingrid, said Erikka, it's just in your head
They'll never be a monster under your bed!

Messages

Whose fortune am I telling today
In the words I speak
Records that I play
Who am I to dance with
On patterns of the mind
Delivering messages
Wrapped in space and time
Energetic scripts
On a green and blue stage
Parts to play
In this infinite parade

Memorable encounters

Some people flit into our lives for just a moment,
some stay a while, others stand a permanent feature
and there are those that come and go.
We may ponder and ask, what was that encounter?
Sometimes we can see a beautiful purpose,
even when encounters are hard.
And then there are those with whom we generously
give and graciously receive, and sometimes one appears missing.
There are no rules, we can gain seemingly the biggest
gifts from the briefest encounters.
The greatest lessons from those despised
and steady love from relationships with great distance.
Are you my friend, my lover, my foe,
acquaintance, comrade, someone I don't yet know.
Are you my future, my past, my now,
my tomorrow, my yesterday, my spoken, my untold.
A part of my story arranged to unfold.
A chapter already written, a treasure map to love.
Whatever you are to me, and I to you,
let us encounter each other with appreciation,
with wisdom and with honour too.

Marriage

Love
 let us share
            honestly
     our worst bits
and best bits
          everything
             in between
     Help us hold
             them all
   our priceless
           collections
    gathered in
by life's
        experiences
Let us Love
    the cracks
          chips and
             faded colour
    our splendid
   vintage
     reminding
each other
    we truly are
  deserving of
Love

Magic and Miracles

The stuff of truth
The stuff that blows our minds
That breaks up our beliefs and concepts
Tears up our assumptions and judgments
Washes out preconceptions
Dusts the dingiest corners of the mind
Reconfigures our neural pathways
Brings joy to the joy-less
And Love into the Love-less
Allows expression of pain to soothe us
Magic and miracles they heal us
Whilst acknowledging our truth
We were never broken anyway

Lucid

Lucid seas
Wash me out
Lay me down
Giving the skies blues
The minerals greens
In visions, in voices
Of who I am
Lay me down
Wash me clean
Lucid seas

Loves me

The hand of my God
Reaching inside me
Rummaging around
Pulling up demons
It looks like suffering
Feels like suffering
Stinks like suffering
I know life is whole
I hear that whispering
In my blood
That feeds the drums
Of my ears

BUT I wail
In my human being
I can only see night
And day
Severally
Still the whispers
Flow just enough
Trickling beautiful
Through me
From somewhere
Unseen
Rooting my trees
In earthly cycles
Of growth and rest

Here come the woodpeckers
Knocking through my bark
Digging the pains
Of my flesh
The stories I've held
Laid down in my rings
The hammered holes
Give freedoms
To demons
The hand of my God
Knows me – loves me
Rummages in me

No exceptions

Love is your truth
And truth
Has no exceptions

Magic

Love is magic
Carry it with you
And generously decorate
Everything you witness
Then watch the world
Fall for Love
And open up

Loosening

A loosening
Between
Where I
And this world
In some way
Cease to make sense
A new view has come
Has lit up
The previously unseen
Perhaps left by the night
Is now clear in the day
And here I find myself
In between

Where chaos reigns
As reshuffling occurs
And off kilter
Not quite understanding
-I'm asking
What this means
For the old story
How to be
With new insights of self
So, I lie in the bath
I garden
I walk

Be blessed
With nature
With friendship
With feeling held
Knowing Love is effervescent
Even when I am not
Life rising into every moment
Still sturdy in the in between
Whatever perception might be
Life is beautifully unfolding
Towards itself
Even in chaos' standing room

While adjustments take place
It's happening – Love
Even without a known outcome
There is outcome
Just underneath
Change is inevitable
And always Love

Listen

Life urging us to listen, to ourselves
words leaving our mouth
Created inside, put together
and constructed by beliefs
experiences of being us
Sometimes these **words**
get directed elsewhere
but are of us. Listen, life **says, listen**

what are you hearing your**self say**
what are you teaching, **about**
your inner working**s**
your inner world. The world
of your speaking, the same world
of your thoughts, holding
the wisdom of you. Your feelings
urging you to listen
more carefully

there is important information
to be heard, to be known
Opportunities constantly, presenting
themselves for expansion
Listen to the world of you
what is alive, in that world
can you use all you are
to experience yet more.

A night

Life
Without noise
Life
Without movement
Existing in between
Sheets
And somewhere else?
Happening
And communicating
Sometimes in ripples
And drips
Easily forgotten
And sometimes in waves
And cascades
Startling us
Our dreams that live
nightly
Still unfolding
Still expressing
Life

Assumptions

Life without assumptions
Can talk to me
Sing to me
Of what it is
Share its wisdom
In the space that exists
Where assumptions do not

Strength

Life Loves me
Life holds me
I AM
The peace
And strength
Of God

Your world

A horrible nightmare
Erupts in your world
Yet you keep choosing Love

Anger is demanded of you
But amidst your confusion
You keep choosing Love

Though you fear that keeping choosing Love
Will expose your soft underbelly
Still you keep choosing Love

Despite all the evidence to the contrary
Nothing can overpower you
If you keep choosing Love

Have confidence that Love's presence
Will guide and keep you safe
As you keep choosing Love

Your Light shines bright
Inspiring and healing
So keep choosing Love

Because there is really nothing else
And it is what you are
Keep choosing Love

By Eric Long

Air

Life astound me
Let me be astounded
May I express this generously
Beautiful draw in with my every breath
Let me breathe beautiful generously
May this be my air

I give

Let there be Joy
 and Freedom
To know everything
 has only
        the meaning
            I give it

I can rejoice
 in this freedom
And find Joy
 in the meaning
            I give

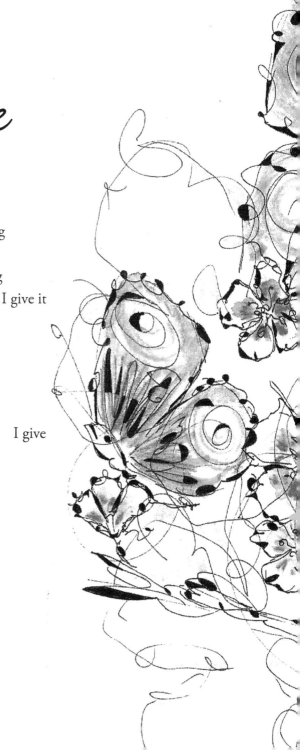

Decorated

All the same
just decorated
in different
patterns
and colours

Myself

It's all inside
The outside
Is all inside
All things outside
Of myself
Exists inside
Myself

No-thing

It's all experience
How would it be
To see nothing as broken
Genuinely no- thing to fix
…Wow
Amen

Surely

It has to be everything
For spirituality to not be a nonsense
It has to be everything
All things spiritual
For God not to be a nonsense
God has to be everything
No exceptions, All included
This window has a different view

Internal monologue

There it is chattering away
Defining what is
Agreeing with what's happening
And disagreeing
Complaining about what isn't
Surely something needs controlling
Confirming and repelling
Talking about what could be changed
Ticking internal boxes
Of expectations
Perceived requirements
Is any of it true
Is any of it real
Or is it just stuff
Debris from life lived
Leftovers from experiences gone by
Dross from excess data
Cluttering my mind

Unnecessarily trying to help
When help is not needed
Trying to keep me safe
When there is no threat
Opportunity for evolution
Moving away from old information
Into the empty space of now
Clearing room for what's being given
What life is endeavouring to give
With no chatter, cluttering me
There is a broader view
Of generous gifts
Being laid on me

Inside is outside

If I'm going into battle with friends
I'm going into battle with myself
If I'm in battle with myself
There will be war
If there is war inside me
There will be war outside of me

Innocence

There was a moment in time
Where guilt showed up
And claimed us
Becoming a ruler over our lives
Then mostly unknowingly
We Act from this inheritance
But that which lived before
Still breathes
Still has a now muffled voice
What happens when life gives
Opportunity after opportunity
To hear more clearly
That inheritance of guilt
Gifting – an asking – a wanting
To know who we were before
And then perhaps we'll gain
Clarity of our innocence
And reinstate this ruler
Giving back and bowing down
To our innocence instead

In

In the flow
- Surrender
The best place I know
Every cell resonating with alive
Engaging in glory
It's a decision
Each moment
To surrender
Each moment
To be here
In the flow
The best place I know
- Surrender

Clearing out

Spring clearing out
Using my imagination
To muck out the old
Making space
For new bedding

In 9

Blind-sided by emotion
I've watched my reaction
I know my trigger
You're upset…
At me
This makes me vulnerable
My personality style
My survival strategy
I'm okay if you're okay
Triggered
Watching my internal script
I'll choose where to go
What to follow
Picking different cues
My internal monologue
How do I want to respond?
What do I wish to write in?
An apology
With ownership
Of my part in this play…

Then I see the shift
The change in your scenery
Yet still my inner workings
Are scouting for danger
Writing your behaviour
As upset with me
So… I'm watching me
The drama of convincing myself
That I am vulnerable
There's still threat
Even though I saw a shift

But here I find myself
This refractory period
I'm in it
But I see it
Myself still flooded with
emotion
Still looking through
Emotion filled spectacles
This limited perspective
Creating stories that match
To get me acting in accordance
And keep myself safe
What tosh this is!

In this moment
There is no danger
Right now
This is old data
Counterproductive
I want to let go
Release the emotion
Come back to an empty stage
Where I see past my personality
My survival strategy
My responding emotions
Return me to peace
An empty floor
Creating new scenery with ease
Some joy
Much appreciation
And Love…

Blessed

I'm so lucky
so utterly blessed
how good life feels
when I notice
all of it - mundane
- small - and that of
everyday life
is rich with blessings
so rich
that suddenly
my blessings feel
overwhelming
I can't hold them
they spill over my edges
like an overflowing jug…

I'm okay

When I don't understand
And not understanding
Feels painful and confusing
What can I do to soothe myself
To ease the burden of not knowing
Can I release myself from the future
Can I leave all pasts in yesterdays
If I reach for only this moment
Forget that there may be another day
Stay here and here only, right now
Only this moment is empty
No woes, worries and grief
Only this moment is forever
Infinitely laden with peace
In this moment I'm bigger
Brighter and lighter and freer
As the infinite explores my cells
Opens them up to all possibilities
Opens them up to myself
Life flowing through this experience
And in this now

I'm okay

I'm curious

Why did you come
What are you surmounting
Would you share with me
Your greatest gift to All
Your fear to over-come
Challenges met head-on
Written into all you do
All you see, who you came to be
Share with me what is held
In your human heart
Your cells, your skin
What you came here to win
The wounds you wanted
To heal, the experiences
You wanted to feel
The light and dark of Love
Would you share with me
The gift you came here to be

New

Just walk the road
perhaps you'll see
what
      the path
           is made
                of

I would rather be in silence,

Be
quiet

than talk without conviction.

I wanted this?

I came here to do this?
I betrayed you to be loyal?
I hated you to grow Love?
I abused you because I care?
I took from you to give?
We suffer to be abundant?

Spending time

I have spent time
Wanting what's been taken
Time to spend time
On what's been given

Whole

I am holistic
bring my pieces
back together
Amen

Meeting me

How many times
Do I sit with myself
And meet myself
Each day?

Home

Create a loving
supportive
safe home
inside yourself
then
you've got it all
and
take it everywhere

Always calling

Heavy moments
Sometimes days
Or weeks
Or a heavy year
Or years
What is the heaviness
And what if its okay
Or more than okay
Challenging us
Pain talking with us
About something
That's been resisted
Or healing needed
It will subside
As Life desired
Is always calling us

good friends

Resistance and suffering
Are forever companions
Sharing creative endeavours
That forge opportunities
Placing them hand in hand

How they dance along paths
Purposefully stepping
Onto those cracks
Chaos their pastime
Upturned stones their relish

Gifting freedoms to critters
That laid dormant in the dark
Knowing their antics
And embellishments
Will bear mixed triumph

Their longing is for each other
Is ferocious and focused
And bears fruit unseen
What a love affair this is
Running through the world's seams

Gone

A zillion-worlds
Being experienced
In a zillion ways
And when I look
Through the eyes
Of this particular one
This perceived moment
Where I think I am
Where you have been
… And gone
My heart breaks and aches
In a crushing agony
That feels indescribable
That reaches depths
That you might imagine
Un-survivable

Yet in my crushed lungs
There is air
I breathe
Without you
And a zillion-different-worlds
Still appear to flow
In and out
Forever changing
Forever being perceived
And it all includes
This one without you
Where by some Miracle
In this wonder
Of experience
I still breathe

Your Gold

Can I mine for Gold
everywhere
in all moments
a baby's laugh
drug-drenched eyes
the seemingly open-hearted
the seemingly underhand

Go Gently

When did feelings become a hindrance
Good to strive for and bad to be resisted
Labelled as wanted or unwelcome
Are feelings bad when we cradle them
Gently holding them as a new born babe
Then are they all loving communication
That we can trust, about our thoughts
And when did thoughts become a hindrance
Labelled as good and bad, helpful and hell-full
If we delicately cradle them as we would a babe
Are they loving communication about our beliefs
And when were we taught to set beliefs in stone
And label them as right-full and wrong-full
Conflict with ourselves and then others
If we hold them gently as a new born babe
Can we see them as loving communication
Of lives lived from different experiences
Stories of perspective that can flow and change
As life itself changes and flows…

god in exploration

These explorations of mountain tops
Valleys carved by ice to sea
Fault lines through lands
Seemingly our outside world

Being explorers of emotional highs
And lows, days of loneliness
Dreams of days to come and those gone
Seemingly our inside world

Explorations of abusive encounter
Desperation and dreadful pain
Wielding, receiving, asking to be saved
Seemingly broken worlds

Exploring abundance and lack
Their intimate relationship
Groaning wealth, impoverished lands
Seemingly one versus the other

Detailed explorers of broken heart
Agony of grief and gaining growth
Counting our losses and treasures
Seemingly banking our hearths – ready

Logging thoughts of exploring
How to tick boxes and long for
Abstain and long for
Seemingly rebel and long for?

Exploration of senses and sensibilities
Physically scintillating, emotionally stifling
Planting out seeds of judgments
Seemingly reaping what we sow

Searching, seeking, traversing
Examining, changing and growing
Myriad Life…

Furrowed

It's hard
To feel the plough
Turn me over
Slicing furrows
Across my hard ground
Upturning my underside
Dazzling them in light
Adjusting to this air

Touched by sun
I feel these deep ridges
Dug through me
Gaping
Leaving me open
Shifted, upended
unsettled

Wanting to resettle
Looking for repose
Back to the ground
How will I restore
Full of new space
Yearning and asking
For planting
Ripe for seeds
That I don't know...

To welcome
The plough
-It's hard

Forever

I've been scared
Standing on the edge of forever
With ragged clothes
And blistered feet
Who am I
Who's standing on the edge
I've asked a thousand times
Who am I
In my mind the answer
Is Love
Love is standing on the edge of
forever
What is Love
A word my mind uses
To describe the indescribable
To give sound to something
That can't be said
It's a rich word
Filled with meaning
Myriad opportunity
For mis-understanding
But yet
It's my word of choice
When asking
And hearing
Who am I

Life does

Follow Life
And be surprised

Astounded
Humbled

Follow Life
In confusion
Discomfort

Follow Life
And be held
Holding you

Whilst Life
Does its thing!

Along

Even if
we're trying
to solve a problem
when there isn't
really a problem
it's all experience
travelling along
this mysterious ride…

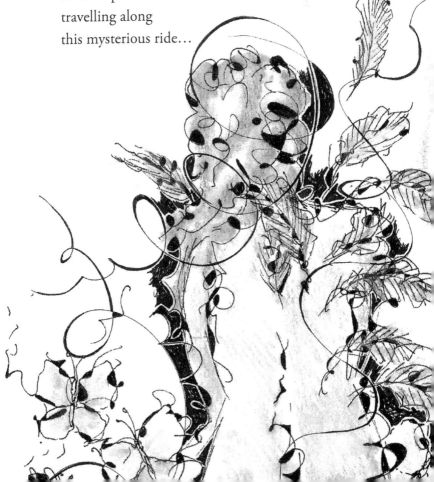

Duelling Emotions

Peaceful Oneness and Wretched Emptiness
Deeply Broken and Wholly Loved
Steady Trust and Wounding Heartache
Debilitating Grief and Gentle Knowing
Joyful Delight and Heavy Longing

The Warriors Dance

Dreams

You speak to me
My nightly dreams
This wonderous Life

Of my unanswered
Unresolved
Inner worlds

You converse
With me
And heal

Crossroads

What can I do
with a crossroad
an idea of choices
differing directions
Yet to be written...
outcomes
Seemingly confused
undecided
What if
such decisions
are already made
because I am...
me
In a quandary
I wonder
I grapple
I mull
I don't know
which way to go
Which path
is better
is right
is for me

What I want
I think
I cannot see
Who am I anyway
already written
in truth?
All decided
mapped out
From a moment
I arrived as me
anything else
I can't be
Then the road
was built
already laid
under these feet
There is no quandary
No not known
as mathematically
all I can be
is me

Closing gaps

I know things
See things
Talk about things
Yet life shows me gaps
Where I'm not being these things

Cinders

When life burns you
Turning you to cinders
Stripping you down to embers
Laid on your hearth
The smoulders lay heavy
Hang thick for a time
As the last of you disappears
In comes a breeze
Smoke spirals heavenward
Clearing and gentle sweeping
There's an unfamiliar view
A new you rising
After these ashes
You don't yet understand
Or know what to do
But all will unfold anyway
You'll break in new shoes
And become acquainted with
Your new and curious attire

Christmas the experience

A yearly opportunity to unwrap
thoughts, feelings and beliefs
for something new to be born…
Are the presents under the tree
repeated, unwanted, regifted
shall I look for something else
under the tree this year…

Pressed Pain

Her cells contracted
Liquid pain squeezed from her eyes
And there is the awareness
A choice sits close
To hold the hand of despair
Never a far reach
Thoughts of hopelessness entice
Feeling its pull of pain
Dropping from her mouth
Her shoulders
Aching her heart
Her gut
Tempted
By safe barriers
That despair offers
It is a mere shuffle
A tiny side step
To the haven of hopelessness
Yet something speaks louder
Not offers of safety
But many offers of Alive
And actually
It's harder to say no to that
Than yes to the other
What a blessing that is
Just enough desire
To feel Alive in living
To keep Love breathing

Caught Between

To be human
We ask
What is it
To be human
My mind ponders
Gathers
Life's contradictions
We say things
Do things
Riddled with holes
A conscious
And unconscious world
Governed by much
Hiding elsewhere
Out of reach
Even in searching
Distant and aloof
My pondering mind
Telling me
To be human
Is caught between
Finite and infinite

To dance with
The contradictions
The painful place
Between
Limited and limitless
Can sense be made
Of such a place
One a dream?
One a reality?
Both with voices
Talking with us
Playing with us
And perceived
In many million ways
Both places
Seemingly abstruse
My mind asks
Are they the same
Just unfathomable
In separation
All transcendental
Experience

The Pool

By the side of the pool, I sat.
Trees, clustering close,
sighed as they gazed at their reflections
perfectly mirrored in the dark water.
A dragonfly shimmering into view
caught my eye, dazzling as it danced.
And then I saw you, slender ash,
your pale trunk a canvas
for the water's art.
Ripples, cast by a trick of light
flow expand contract,
hypnotic as they kiss and play
across your surface
and turn your solid mass
to something liquid.
Tree becomes reflection, reflected
refraction
in hypnotic echo.
And the world shifts
as air and water lift the veil
unmasking what is real
is only maya's face

By Kath Sunderland

Bonne Nuit

Go to sleep, I'll hold your hand
By your side is where I stand

Ever loving, I sing your song
You'll hear my words
And know, that you belong

Here you lie, light and free
When you trust, I stand next to thee

A heart full of faith, is a heart that knows
Where Love is and how Love grows

Go to sleep, I'll hold your hand
By your side, always I stand

Bring intimate

into everything
every moment
all experience
move toward
intimate
welcome
holding, cherished
touching, allowing
knowing
warmth
tender, gentle
grace

intimate
has loving eyes
and delicate strength
intimate
can cast mirrors
without breaking them
see beyond behaviour
and reconcile with lost
it gifts us
soft pillows
to break falls
and balm
to ease abrasions
and cuts

time can stop
with intimate
holding moments
suspended
in other worlds
gentle worlds
creating unknown land
for new experience
with
shared currency
so much power
in bringing
intimate
to every moment

Blank slate

Bring a blank slate
To every moment
Free of the last
Free of anything
That's perceived
To have happened
Yes, it did exist
In a different moment
Not in this one
Every moment
A blank slate
Starting with nothing
Every moment
Can be born
With no thing
And no forward

All I might need
Will be given
In each moment
No need to carry
Any thing
No need to set
A future
Parading forwards
With guesses
I can be empty
And exist
In every moment
With a blank slate

Binsey

Your 360
Surrenders my soul
Your silence digging deep
Ancient layers
Unravelling mine
You know nothing of time

       Our familiarity
       Holds me close
       Your unseen movement
       Slowing my pace
       Arresting my heart
       Taking falsehoods apart

              What is this trust
              I give to you
              Open, Willing, Real
              Yes, I see
              You Give
              Yet ask nothing of me

beautiful world

Can I speak of a more beautiful world
Do you call me naïve for imagining
Wonders that seem impossible
Do you think me foolish
For believing in a place
Where violence does not exist
And this place is already known
Inside us, in our heart's imagination
Someone must be courageous enough
To allow these imaginings to run free
Alternatively, violence
Is what we'll continue to see

Beneath

The Unremembered
That lives inside
Has it built a home
Planning the long stay
Decorating me
Moulding my stance
Influencing my gait
Did it sign a contract
Is there an end date
Will it pack up and leave
Move on and redesignate
Space for healing
Change – change is inevitable
Created by being shown
Something else
The opposite
Of our residents
Remembered or not
Love lives in here too
Being all that exists
Love is decorating too

And when old residents leave
However long they resided
Love has new wallpaper
And fresh paint
Decoration is life lived
And Love is always present
Waiting with a paintbrush

Another Year

and yet   another year   without you
          does time heal   but this is   yet another year
     of aching ripples   and broken heart views

I'll collect more time   as time it seems   moves
          holding more   without you's
but how do I hold more   without you's

and how does gathering more   heal
     when more years   more time   without you
     are sharp hooks   that I feel

in my heart   yes   you always sustain
     but   gathering without you's
  do so   heavily remain

gaining weight   as time exists
               this human life
  where physical   is so painfully   missed

Maybe

Acceptance is friends
with freedom
they hang out together
maybe they get a coffee
maybe they sit in silence
maybe they party til dawn.

Another meeting

I look at you
In your eyes
And I can see
A reflection of me
I'm meeting myself
And you have no choice
You have to give me
To Me
And I'm sure there is
Agreement
That this is so
What we do
For each other
To grow
Expanding worlds
We reflect
What we see

Giving away my secrets
I hide from myself
Good and bad
Light and dark
All opportunity
To be given to
And know
When I accept
Your gift
My reflection
Inside you
There is a beautiful me
Reflected by you
In wonderous eyes
You'll find yourself
I'm reflecting you too

Am I

Am I a storage container?
That holds all my years
And eons of life
Inside
Layers of mud and silt
Deposited over me
As tides wax and wane
Through my life
As salty tears leave dregs
And crabby creations bite
Wounds still bleeding
On broken shells
How do I carry it all
And walk with grains
Of shifting sand
Between my toes

Or
Am I an empty container?
Recreating in every moment
A new ocean
A fresh view
If it seems fossilised and grey
If this moment is made
From elderly friends
Finding reused paper bags
On my beach
They are my patterns
Of thoughts
I'm bringing along
To each new picnic
Every empty moment
Filled with the same sandwiches
Might I bring
An empty container instead…

Agony

It separates you from your soul
Clenching your teeth
And binding your bones
Paralysed by its weight
A hot red iron tail
You're in its coil
Dragged down
Away from colour
To blackness
The dream of oblivion
There is no sense
Pointless, emptiness
Wretched, emptiness
Unbearable, emptiness
Your chest heaves for air
Though you don't want it
It expands anyway
Life still infiltrating you
Leave me alone!
Life, leave me alone
But life does not
Leave you alone
Life lives
In agony

Life says yes
To connection
To prising open your teeth
And breaking binds
Life excels in teaching
You to walk again
Time and time again
Life's agenda for experience
May be beyond
Your understanding
Seemingly in discord
With your expectations
But always taking through you
Another breath
Of unfathomable
Expansive encounter

A more beautiful world

As long as we are at war
With ourselves
We will be at war
With each other

Our relationship with self
Is our world
It is our relationship
With this world

If there are battles
We create battles
If there are judgments
They will be judged

Arrogance to feel worthy
Springs rivers of unworthy
Control to dampen fear
Creates bears of fear raging

What is this self
We're in relationship with
Is there any truth
In truth that is not shared

What foundations exist
Underneath this façade
How deep the substratum
Where we exist together

What holds this ground
Underneath the separate self
Where we could find ourselves
Liberating a more beautiful world

Spot of time

Raging, running, roaring, rushing
Racing past
Its dark waters fly by me

The terrible strength
Erodes banks and fells trees
It leaves them in its wake
For all to see

And surrounding it are jutting rocks
Smoothed pebbles and countless hidden treasures
Fields and pastures coloured green
Beyond that is the sea

Through all of this
Its waters flow, oblivious
Dutifully they run on
Towards the ocean

And though all of this
Make it seem rough and tough
Down by its banks, through tangled trees
I still find it brings peace and happiness to me

By Erikka Ellen Messenger

Meditation

Life is a meditation
Rich with labels
That I can choose
To meditate on

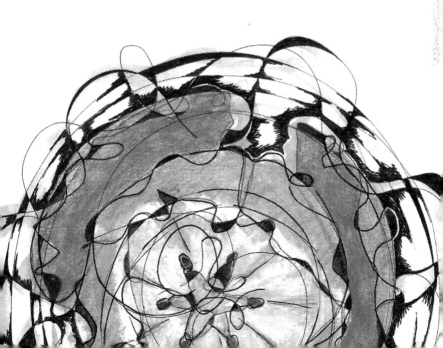

About the Author

Writing has always featured in Catriona's life, having been inspired by her poetic grandmother. Not only is it Catriona's favourite way to express herself, it is a safe place to explore inner worlds. Catriona is sure that all the answers to her questions about life, are hiding inside herself. She finds inspiration in the joy of nature and stillness, and in the discomfort of noise and busyness, and has come to realise that it's all communication. She is inspired every day by the stream of thoughts and feelings she experiences, and the awareness of which ones she wants to follow and give life to.

Catriona joined a creative writing group in 2017 called Mungrisdale Writers, and other than writing poems for her children when they were young, this was the first time she had shared her poems with others. Writing supported her greatly in her most challenging time, the passing of her 13-year-old daughter, and continues to do so.

Catriona fell in love with ink pens and drawing in her teens and even though over the years she has experimented with many creative ideas, she is always drawn back to this first love. She grew up in Cumbria and continues to live there, happily surrounded by family, friends and pets, hills, trees, rivers and wildlife. A favourite pastime is being out and about with her Border Terrier, Miri.

Also by Turquoise Quill Press

For every perceived failure, a zillion expanded worlds
Edges become blurry, as all becomes one
Grace is substantial, the rest will fade
Only Love. always Loved
Falling in Love with myself
We are the Heavens in drops of Gold

Hope Dealer is a book of poetry and illustrations by
Catriona Messenger.
Turquoise Quill Press is an imprint of
Not From This Planet.

NotFromThisPlanet.co.uk